Cryptocurrency

Investment Strategies in 2018

© Copyright 2018

All rights reserved.

The contents of this book may not be reproduced, duplicated or transmitted without direct written permission from the author.

Under no circumstances will any legal responsibility or blame be held against the publisher for any reparation, damages, or monetary loss due to the information herein, either directly or indirectly.

Legal Notice:

You cannot amend, distribute, sell, use, quote or paraphrase any part or the content of this book without the consent of the author.

Disclaimer Notice:

Please note the information contained in this document is for educational and entertainment purposes only. No warranties of any kind are expressed or implied. Readers acknowledge that the author is not engaging in the rendering of legal, financial, medical or professional advice. Please consult a licensed professional before attempting any techniques outlined in this book.

By reading this document, the reader agrees that under no circumstances are the author responsible for any losses, direct or indirect, which are incurred as a result of the use of information contained within this document, including, but not limited to, — errors, omissions, or inaccuracies.

Table of Contents

- Introduction 1
- Chapter One 3
  - History Of Cryptocurrency 3
  - Early Experiments With The Virtual Currencies 3
  - 2008 Economic Crisis And The Birth Of Cryptocurrency 5
  - World Of Crypto Coins – Altcoins 6
  - Blooming Era For Cryptocurrencies 7
- Chapter Two 9
  - What Is Cryptocurrency? 9
  - Cryptocurrency – A Brief Outline 10
  - Finite Supply – Rewards And Risks 11
  - How Do Cryptocurrencies Work? 12
  - Blockchain 13
  - Private Keys 14
  - Wallets 14
  - Miners 15
  - Cryptocurrency Exchanges 17
- Chapter Three 18
  - Why Cryptocurrency? Pros And Cons 18
  - Why Cryptocurrency? 19
  - Pros And Cons Of The Virtual Currency 20
    - Fraudulence 20
    - Anonymity 21
    - Instant Agreement 21
    - Globally Available 21
    - Less Fees 21
    - Owner 22
    - Stringent Regulation By Law 22
    - Possible Venue For Money Laundering 22
    - Data Loss Will Mean Monetary Loss 23
    - Market Volatility 23
    - Irreversible 23
- Chapter Four 25
  - Crypto Coins And Their Potential In Investment 25
  - Crypto Coins Or Altcoins 26
    - Ethereum 26
    - Ripple 27
    - Stellar 28
    - Iota 28
    - Litecoin 29

- Neo 29
- Things To Be Done Before You Start With Your Cryptocurrency Investment Portfolio 30
  - Cryptocurrency Exchange 31
  - Cryptocurrency Wallets 32
- Chapter Five 33
  - Investing In Cryptocurrency 33
  - What % Of The Investment Allocation Should Be Put In Cryptocurrencies? 34
  - How To Choose The Right Cryptocurrency? 35
    - Will I Be Able To Maintain My Capital Amount? 35
    - Does The Coin I Have Chosen Have A Long-Term Plan? 35
    - Will The Coin Help With Safety Benefits? 35
    - Is Your Exit Strategy Ready? 36
  - Ways To Make Money! 36
    - Buy And Hold 36
    - Trading With Margin (Short-Term) 36
    - Mining 37
    - Arbitraging With Cryptocurrencies 37
  - How To Start With Bitcoin Investment? 38
  - Securing The Cryptocurrencies 39
- Chapter Six 40
  - Cryptocurrency Investment Strategies 40
  - Investment Strategy For Cryptocurrency 40
  - Steps To Be Followed For The Right Investment Strategy 42
    - Working Out On The Right Plan To Start Your Investment Portfolio 43
    - Be Ready To Accept The 'Price Dips' 43
    - Securing The Cryptocurrencies 44
  - Making Money 45
    - When To Use The Dips? 46
    - When To Sell? 46
  - Inspiration From A Bitcoin Millionaire 47
- Chapter Seven 49
  - Cryptocurrency Exchanges 49
  - How To Choose The Right Cryptocurrency Exchange? 50
  - Why Is It Important To Choose A Safe Cryptocurrency Exchange? 51
  - Don't Make These Investment Mistakes 52
- Conclusion 55

INTRODUCTION

I would like to take this opportunity to thank you for purchasing this book: *"Cryptocurrency: Investment strategies in 2018."*

The acceptance of cryptocurrency has grown, as the technical literacy of the population is increasingly high making it possible for more people to learn and explore this digital currency. The booming rise in its value has motivated the majority of tech-savvy professionals to try their luck with cryptocurrencies. Social media newsfeeds carry more and more news related to cryptocurrencies adding on to the curiosity of the commoners. I was one among them until I heard about Bitcoins and other popular crypto coins. These digital coins saved me when I was almost completely bankrupt, and I take this chance to thank my friend who introduced me to these virtual currencies. The small investment I made in Bitcoin helped me journey towards the seat of a millionaire. Within a year, I started playing with the cryptocurrencies, and by the year-one, I had close to a million in my piggy bank.

How did I do it? Is it really possible? Yes! But you should take all the necessary steps to learn about the cryptocurrencies – the history, the technology it uses and the different ways to invest before you decide to choose the coin that will best suit you. The reason I am writing this is I want to help readers to try and make a fortune with cryptocurrencies – the way I did. The primary objective of the book is to give you a brief on how to invest in cryptocurrency and to help you understand the potential of the right cryptocurrency investment.

The chapters will concentrate on the history of cryptocurrency, the underlying technology the digital currency uses, the different cryptocurrencies that are available in the crypto market and the different investment strategies that can be followed. The book will also make you realize the importance of cryptocurrency, the pros and cons of investing in cryptocurrency, etc.

I hope this book will help you with an in-depth understanding of cryptocurrency and the various options available to invest in the said digital currency to start your journey towards the road of becoming a millionaire.

Thank you once again for purchasing the book. I hope you have an interesting and informative read!

Good luck!

CHAPTER ONE

History of Cryptocurrency

Until yesterday, the only currency people across the globe accepted and acknowledged as the kind they could hold physically – the pieces of paper which had their country's currency printed on and referred as 'fiat currencies.' Today, they are amazed at the thought of virtual currency that comes with the idea of storing value digitally, giving it a name – Cryptocurrency. Though it is difficult to digest this straight away, the concept has gradually gained acceptance among the majority of people as they start to appreciate the fact that a decade of reasonable thinking, mathematical research and the strong instinctive attempts to primarily change the world's long-existing centrally controlled financial order. And this by itself is a gargantuan task that will take a definite amount of time to get accepted entirely.

Early experiments with the virtual currencies

Before the concept of cryptocurrencies entered the market in 2009, there were many failed attempts by merchants and business enterprises in virtual currency since from as early as the 1980s. Initially, commercial businesses offered virtual currency to their customers in the form of a token, which acted as a representation in fiat currencies. People could use these virtual tokens to purchase products or store as credits or transfer to other people, etc.

David Chaum, the American cryptographer, invented the first form of virtual currency – DigiCash as an extension to the popular encryption algorithm RSA in the Netherlands. It had an interesting product – eCash that gained media attention along with its incredible technology for which Microsoft was ready to offer $180 million to the cryptographer's company. The Windows giant wanted to put DigiCash on every PC, which had their operating system. DigiCash became a failure when the cryptographer took the wrong decision of not accepting Microsoft's offer adding on to various other mistakes. It, in fact, caught the antagonistic attention of the Netherlands Central Bank and led to its ultimate bankruptcy in 1998.

The next wave of web-based currency leapt from the earlier failures, and many startups brought in payment solutions and virtual money systems, but none created an impact and then came 'PayPal.' They had a clear objective and understood what the users wanted – they offered a flawless peer-to-peer payment transfer method, which is still the best-sorted transaction mode among vendors.

E-Gold was the next attempt, which followed the footprints of PayPal and started offering gold credits or eGold by accepting physical gold deposits from their users. Good volume of cross-border payments and trade happened, but it, unfortunately, had to shut down due to counterfeit high-yielding investing program, scams and Ponzi schemes.

2008 Economic crisis and the birth of cryptocurrency

The world economy saw a dangerous threat in its history when the 2008 economic crisis hit the USA becoming a checkpoint to analyze global finance and its technology. It was indeed an eye-opener for the insensitive conduct that had leaked into the crusaders of the finance world. This led to the emergence of Satoshi Nakamoto and his idea of a decentralization concept. A white paper was published at the end of 2008, which mentioned about the blockchain concept – the source code and the technology, and the first cryptocurrency – Bitcoin was introduced in early 2009.

This invention laid the foundation of the new technology, which challenged to replace all types of central authority with a decentralized, peer-to-peer, and open source trust protocol. Today we have 16 million Bitcoins circulating in the cryptocurrency market generating a total market capitalization of close to $50 billion. The interesting part is that the concept of cryptocurrency is gaining popularity among users, developers and business communities alike. There are quite a few countries such as Canada, Japan and Australia who have already regulated Bitcoin under their taxation frameworks and Bitcoins have been accepted by law.

World of crypto coins – Altcoins

Since the introduction of Bitcoin in 2009, the digital world started to see more cryptocurrencies, also known as altcoins or crypto tokens. These new coins used the same technology – blockchain technology used by Bitcoin with improved features that Bitcoin couldn't offer. They started to call themselves an 'alternative to Bitcoin' and hence are referred as Altcoins. Today, there are close to 1000 cryptocurrencies that are being traded globally by many crypto enthusiasts with the total market capitalization crossing over $100 billion.

Ether, Litecoin, Ripple, Monero, Zcash, Dash, and Stratis are few of the popularly used crypto coins. This resulted in an entirely new trading industry – Cryptocurrency trading on a global scale. Many new applications used blockchain technology and cryptocurrency became their token. A separate online marketplace was developed which enabled cryptocurrency buyers and sellers to communicate on crypto transactions, and they were referred as 'Cryptocurrency exchanges.'

Ethereum became the next popular cryptocurrency after Bitcoin and also referred to itself as the 'silver to Bitcoin's gold.' Vitalik Buterin proposed the new Ethereum platform in late 2013 that was taken live in July 2015. Ethereum offered an open source platform, which runs on blockchain, based computing technology with the following features:

- Smart contracts (Allowing developers and users the scripting functionality to create contractual agreements)

- Ethereum Virtual Machine (Comprehensive virtual machine)
- dApps (Decentralized applications – set of programming languages to create your own blockchain apps)

The Ethereum platform was fueled by its crypto token 'Ether (ETH),' and within a short period, it showed its dominance as it received huge support from developers, businesses and users. This open source blockchain platform has helped many startups to create their own crypto tokens that are built on the Ethereum platform. Ethereum's total market cap value touched $30 billion.

The major reasons for Ethereum's popularity are:

- Size of the developers' community
- Easy to develop
- Technical edge it provides over other blockchain platforms
- Enterprise Ethereum Alliance (Association of world's leading businesses which utilize and help the Ethereum platform)

Blooming era for Cryptocurrencies

When it comes to finance and trade, the concept of cryptocurrencies has already started breaking many barriers and borders inviting more people into its world. There are already close to a thousand coins which are competing against each other when the blockchain development is still it its budding phase.

There may come a time when a single boss will erupt out from the sea of cryptocurrencies followed by few leading crypto coins. They might define their own trend when it comes to payments, trading, investing, global banking infrastructures, etc. These virtual currencies might gain popularity in such a way that the entire mainstream will be forced to adopt applications based on blockchain technology.

CHAPTER TWO

What is Cryptocurrency?

As of today's date, the exciting concept of 'Cryptocurrency' has the power to alter the global finance for a better economic status but with the 'work in progress,' tag on its technology, the control on currency production and the current fiscal policy still appear to be secure. It is important for cryptocurrency enthusiasts and the other majority who are fascinated by the digital currency's promise to be aware of the concept's practical limitations.

If you come across a particular cryptocurrency that claims to provide total anonymity or resistance from legal liability, it is better to think twice before getting into investment opportunities with such coins, as they are worthy of deep cynicism. Gold is often advertised as the ultimate inflation hedge in the economic market, but they are still subject to crazy volatility when compared to many other fiat currencies.

Let us try to understand this virtual currency in detail so that it will be easy when you decide to invest in them. What is Cryptocurrency? They are digital entries, which provide 'means of exchange' during transactions created and used by individuals or groups. This virtual currency is not regulated by any government body and is considered as an alternative means of financial exchange that is out of bounds of the respective state's monetary policy.

Cryptocurrency — a brief outline

Complex cryptographic protocols are used to encrypt sensitive data during the transaction process by securing their exchange units, and Cryptocurrency works on this protocol. The developers build these protocols using an advanced mathematical technique, which makes it completely impossible to break the encrypted data. This leaves the hackers with no chance to duplicate or fake the secured cryptocurrencies.

Apart from securing the transactions, the protocol is also responsible for hiding the identity of the users making it difficult to trace the flow of the funds and the owner of the transaction. Cryptocurrency provides anonymity to the transactional process and to the participants involved. The decentralized concept of cryptocurrency confirms its supply and value to be controlled by complex cryptographic protocols built into their source codes thereby making it unfeasible for the government regulatory bodies or central banks to determine or influence the virtual currency with external decisions.

The miner's play a crucial role to ensure the functionality of the cryptocurrency works stably and swiftly. Miners are cryptocurrency users, who use huge amounts of computing power to document transactions, validate them and accept new crypto tokens and verification fees offered in return for their role's purpose.

It is also possible to exchange cryptocurrencies with fiat currencies (USD, GBP, EURO, YEN, INR, etc.) with variable exchange rates in unique online marketplaces known as Cryptocurrency exchange. These exchanges are to some extent susceptible to hacking and are said to be the most common 'venue' for crypto coin theft. It is therefore essential to choose the right, reliable and prominently used the exchange to avoid such risks.

Finite supply – rewards and risks

Most of the cryptocurrencies have a limited supply to their coin generation, i.e., the source codes of these virtual currencies are outlined with logical protocols which have a defined number of crypto units that can and will ever exist – the supply is finite. With time, it will become difficult for the miners to generate more crypto coins as the mining difficulty goes up and once the upper limit of the units has been reached, then the coins cannot be 'mined' any further as the limit is over. Bitcoin's limit is 21 million, and it has already reached 16 million units.

The digital currency's finite supply makes them deflationary similar to gold and other valuable stones – which have limited supply – when compared to fiat currencies (as central banks can produce an unlimited supply of new currencies based on government directives – in theory). But not all cryptocurrencies are finite; there are few that don't fall under this category, as they are pre-mined.

The impassable data security and the political independence allow cryptocurrency users to gain benefits which are not possible for fiat currency users and the financial systems that support these traditional currencies. For example, it is easily possible for a government to freeze or seize a traditional bank account in its control but it is impossible to do the same thing with cryptocurrency funds even if the holder is a legal resident or the country's citizen.

When there are rewards, the possibility of risk is also higher in such areas. Similarly, this virtual currency has its own set of risks and downside – price value volatility and illiquidity, which doesn't affect the fiat currencies to a large extent. The anonymity feature that the cryptocurrency provides has led to its frequent usage in black market transactions forcing many countries to view the concept with absolute hostility and distrust. Though few advocate the new currency to be a potential alternate investment source, few finance experts look at them as just speculations.

How do Cryptocurrencies work?

Though the source codes and technical features that support and protect crypto coins are extremely complicated, it isn't that difficult to understand the basic functionality of the technology to become an informed cryptocurrency user. Most of the new cryptocurrencies that are available in the market are 'just variations on Bitcoins with new add-on features.' The cryptocurrencies express their value in units' which is similar to fiat currencies, i.e., similar to $20 (which is 20 US dollars), it is 20 BTC (which is 20 Bitcoins).

Various concepts administer the values of cryptocurrency alongside its security and reliability. We will get into the details to understand how it works.

Blockchain

The blockchain is the distributed public master ledger which records and stores all the transactional activities after validating the authenticity of the transaction and its ownership to the currency's exchange units at any given point in time. The entire transactional history until the date is recorded to a finite length that increases every time a new transaction request is initiated. Every node in the cryptocurrency network stores the entire history of the transaction by making ledger entries of the identical copies of the blockchain in their respective 'single ledger.'

What is a cryptocurrency network? It is the network of decentralized server nodes run by tech-savvy individuals or group referred by the name 'miners' who keep recording and authenticating all the cryptocurrency transactions continuously. The transaction isn't verified and finalized; until it is stamped and appended to the blockchain that is usually done by the miners within minutes (ten minutes approximately).

The transaction is irreversible once it is confirmed and unlike conventional payment providers, such as credit cards and PayPal, the cryptocurrencies have no chargeback functions or built-in refund options – so if you have made the wrong transaction, it is done, there is no way to reverse it. But there are few new cryptocurrencies that are offering basic refund features – though this is not clear yet.

When the transaction is 'in process'; i.e., between initialization and finalization, the cryptocurrencies cannot be used by either of the party, therefore, solving the problem of double spending. Double spending is using the same currency unit for transactions more than once.

Private Keys

If you own a cryptocurrency, you will have a private key that authenticates your identity and allows you to exchange units. This private key comprises of random numbers formatted as whole numbers between 1 and 78 digits long. You can acquire and spend cryptocurrency once you have your private key. It is not possible to perform any transactions without the private key, i.e., if you lose or misplace your private key, you will not be able to do anything with the crypto coins that you have stored in your coin wallet – your crypto assets are as good as useless without the private key.

Though this feature provides intense security to your cryptocurrency, it is equally harsh as losing your private key will indicate that you have just burnt your own cash and there is no way to recover it. You can create another private key and start gathering cryptocurrency all over again, but you cannot get back your crypto coins secured by your lost key.

Wallets

Every cryptocurrency user will have a wallet confirming them as the temporary owners of their respective currency units. These wallets will have unique information – such as wallet address. The private keys substantiate the legitimacy of the cryptocurrency transaction, and the wallets reduce the risk of thefts for stored coins that aren't being used. When a cryptocurrency is purchased, it needs to be stored in a location until it is used for transactional purposes and wallets are the place where it can be stored.

Online wallets that cryptocurrency exchanges use are prone to hackers, due to security breaches. Mt. Gox, the popular Bitcoin exchange, was declared bankrupt and shut down when hackers stole more than $450 million worth of Bitcoins. There are different types of wallets – online, offline, hardware, paper wallets, etc.

You can store coin wallets on an external storage device, an internal hard drive or on the cloud. Irrespective of the type of wallet you decide to use, it is always advisable to take a backup of the .dat file (the file that holds the cryptocurrency). It doesn't mean that you are duplicating the actual cryptocurrency units but just recording their existence and the current ownership of the wallet.

Miners

Miners are the indirect governors of the cryptocurrencies' value and act as record keepers for the crypto communities. The miners use advanced technical processes to verify the comprehensiveness, safety and accuracy of the cryptocurrencies' blockchain. The miners invest on huge computational processors, private server farms with mining rigs, mining pools, and mining software applications to mine a crypto coin. The miners sometimes work as individuals or form a mining community comprising of dozens of individuals.

Miners verify new transaction requests by solving cryptographic puzzles, updating them to the central ledger and adding them to the list of existing blockchain. Each verified transaction is known as a 'block.' The blocks comprise all the executed transactions since the recently verified one – therefore adding on to the existing blockchain. The term 'miner' associates to the fact that the work of a miner is to create wealth in the form of new cryptocurrency units.

When a new transaction is verified, the miner receives a monetary reward, two rewards in fact – fixed number of newly mined crypto coins and a variable number of existing coin collected as a transaction fee, which is paid by the buyers (less than 1% of the transaction value). Hence, cryptocurrency mining is considered as a lucrative business for passive income if you are ready to invest in power (electricity) and the hardware (mining rig).

As per the source code, the cryptocurrencies will automatically adjust to the amount of mining power while working on creating the new blockchain copies, i.e., verifying the new transaction requests. But when the transaction request increases, then the mining difficulty goes higher making it a bit tough for the miners to confirm the verification. In such cases, the miners take a longer time to verify the transaction, so the flow of new transaction requests goes down, therefore, making the mining difficulty low again.

The ultimate objective is to keep the average interval time between new transaction verification at a predetermined level. Example: the average mining time for Bitcoin is ten minutes, and for ether, it is 15 seconds.

Cryptocurrency Exchanges

Cryptocurrency exchanges are online marketplaces, which allow the cryptocurrency buyers and senders to communicate directly to buy or sell their own crypto coins. These exchange platforms allow the users to exchange their cryptocurrency for fiat money or other crypto coins. They charge less than 1% of the transaction value as their fee.

These exchanges play an important role when it comes to generating liquid markets for the leading cryptocurrencies and also help in fixing their value relative to fiat currencies. After the collapse of the exchange 'Mt. Gox', the cost value of the exchange rates is exceedingly volatile. There was a 50% decrease in Bitcoin's US dollar exchange rate when the Japan-based cryptocurrency exchange crumpled.

There are less popular cryptocurrencies whose liquidity and the price value is still low compared to the fiat currencies or other popular cryptocurrencies. These coins can be exchanged only through private peer-to-peer transfers. Cryptocurrencies such as Bitcoin can trade on special secondary exchanges that are similar to traditional forex exchanges. These secondary exchange platforms allow the cryptocurrency users to exchange their crypto coins for fiat currencies such as USD, Euro, etc. and can also be traded with other crypto coins (inclusive of less popular cryptocurrencies).

CHAPTER THREE

Why Cryptocurrency? Pros and Cons

The evolution of cryptocurrency in the 'fiat currency' dominated economy came up as a revolution when it almost challenged the transaction functionality and the governing style of the central banks or government authorized body after the 2008 financial fiasco. The concept of cryptocurrency and the technology it used almost took control of the money away from the government – it was impulsive according to the financial experts. Since the first cryptocurrency 'Bitcoin' became popular and started getting acknowledged by various tech-savvy financial market players (investors and traders), the fad for cryptocurrency grew more, and there are few reasons behind the same:

- 'Getting rich quick': more people were attracted to this idea
- 'The thrill of keeping up with the trend': many didn't want to lose out on the opportunity
- 'Behind the scene activity for drug dealers and tax evaders': though Bitcoin is still traceable compared to the other crypto coins
- 'Attraction to steadfast store of value': increase in price value at remarkable speed

Though the cryptocurrency market is considered to be extremely volatile and unpredictable, it is still going strong among crypto enthusiasts only because of its underlying technology – blockchain. This technology offers more to the users and is not restricted only to cryptocurrencies.

The financial world is 100 percent full of fiat currencies, and the idea of computer-generated digital currency is innovative and a bit revolutionary in the aspect of taking the creation and control of money away from the government.

Why Cryptocurrency?

The thing that makes this concept of cryptocurrency amazing is that the currency 'Bitcoin' is of limited quantity and will become scarce soon making it function more like gold or other precious metals/stones. The demand and value are more when the product is scarce or limited. It is only possible to mine 21 million Bitcoins, and anything more than that is completely impractical – that is how the code is written. There are already 16 million Bitcoins in circulation currently and once the miners reach their upper limit in few years, they cannot be mined anymore, i.e., the total denomination in circulation rapidly approaches a fixed mathematical limit.

Let us imagine a globally accepted safe cryptocurrency with its value not getting subjected to purposefully organized crumble with a finite supply and universally accepted coins with its production beyond the control of any particular government body. Wouldn't that be wonderful? Yes! That is what the blockchain technology can offer -

not only with cryptocurrencies but also with various other applications.

It is crucial to understand the pros and cons of a particular technology before finalizing your decision to invest in the respective stock – weighing the good and bad! Cryptocurrency is a combination of innovation and technology – the technology is already creating a storm among the tech-savvy experts, but it is all about the acceptance from the entire crowd that is needed. With more countries and their government trying their best to research and understand about this new digital currency, we can expect a change very soon.

Pros and Cons of the virtual currency

Wordpress became the first vendor to accept Bitcoin as payment in late 2012. After this huge change, many big names – Microsoft, Expedia, an online electronics retailer Newegg.com gave their consumers an option of new payment mode – 'Bitcoin.' Today most online vendors have started to view cryptocurrencies as a legal payment method. Apart from Bitcoin, there are few other crypto coins that are also accepted for commercial payments, and exchanges allow the users to exchange the crypto coins for fiat currencies or Bitcoins. This increases the flexibility and provides critical liquidity.

Advantages of Cryptocurrencies

Fraudulence
Cryptocurrency is a digital coin and does not allow the sender to fake transactions similar to the 'chargebacks that happen in credit cards/.'

Anonymity

The blockchain technology used in cryptocurrencies provides anonymity to the user and his transactions. The 'hash' algorithm used in the cryptocurrency masks the identity of the sender and the transaction data, therefore, making it impossible to track the details. It operates on 'push' mechanism.

Instant agreement

The blockchain technology allows the developers or users to create 'contracts' or 'agreements' based on their requirements and triggers the contracts automatically with respect to the input value. For instance, to buy a property using traditional methods; one will have to involve a notary or lawyer (third parties) to pay or register the real estate. The 'smart contracts' in Ethereum platform have the power to eliminate the intervention of third parties by designing and customizing the digital contract in such a way that it automatically completes the traditional asset transfers without manual intervention of external factors.

Globally available

Since cryptocurrency is completely powered by the Internet, it is accessible and available globally to all the users in the digital world. Based on the country and the current location, any Internet user can get access to cryptocurrency exchange platforms to buy their first crypto coin and begin their investment process.

Less Fees

The cryptocurrency exchanges usually don't charge any transaction fees as the miners are already compensated by the network for their work (verifying the transaction requests). Though there is no transaction fee for cryptocurrency transactions, most of the beginners in cryptocurrency investment will engage a third-party service (secondary cryptocurrency exchange) such as Coinbase to create and maintain their own crypto wallet during the trading process. You can compare these exchanges to PayPal, which provides peer to peer online cash transfers between parties.

Owner

Cryptocurrency is the only exclusive electronic digital cash system, which makes you the sole owner of your crypto coin. You buy a coin; then you own it – the coin, the private key, the related public key that creates your crypto address – everything! No one can take the cryptocurrency away from you unless you lose it.

For instance, when you own a PayPal account, you don't actually own it; you are just a user or the account holder of the electronic cash system. If the company thinks that your account has been compromised, they can freeze all the assets without giving you a prior warning. It is up to you to go behind them and do whatever is needed to access your funds in the account.

<u>Disadvantages of Cryptocurrencies</u>

Stringent regulation by law

The anonymity of the transactions will force the government bodies to take stringent measures to control the cryptocurrency usage, as tax evasion is a major concern. The capital gains made from cryptocurrency investment are also subjected to tax (recent inclusion in law). Few countries had gone to the extent of banning cryptocurrency entirely to prevent money laundering.

Possible venue for money laundering

The biggest disadvantage of cryptocurrency is its regulatory concern as it has the capacity to assist in illegal activity – grey and black-market denomination in Bitcoin and other popular crypto coins. Example: Silk Road – the well-known dark-web marketplace used cryptocurrencies for illicit drug transactions and other illegal activity before it was shut down in 2014. Besides this, people use cryptocurrency market to convert their 'black money' into 'white money' and clean up their mess to mask its source.

Data loss will mean monetary loss

When cryptocurrency users are not cautious and avoid taking the necessary safety measures to evade data loss, they irreversibly suffer financial loss. Example: If a cryptocurrency user purchases his Bitcoin and stores it in a hardware wallet but doesn't take the necessary steps to save his private key in a secured place or forgot to take a backup of the already stored private key (in a physical storage device), then he will suffer permanent financial loss when the device is stolen or hacked.

Market volatility

The remarkable increase in the price value and an equally steep decrease in price value make the cryptocurrency market extremely volatile. If the investor doesn't devise a proper strategy or make a smart exit plan when needed, he or she might get emotionally stressed with the unpredictability in the market.

Irreversible

When the transaction is confirmed, there is no possibility of reversing the same in cryptocurrency, i.e., if you sent a Bitcoin to a wrong Bitcoin address, then it is gone there is no possible way for you to get it back unless the recipient sends it by himself. Similarly, if you become a victim of theft because you had stored your crypto coin in online cryptocurrency exchanges without strong security (stronger passwords or two-factor authentication), then it is entirely your fault that you lost the coin.

Though cryptocurrency is exciting with the power to change the global economy, it has a long way to go to mature its stand regarding liquidity and mass acceptance. For now, it is the responsibility of the cryptocurrency users to have an in-depth understanding of the concept, its limitations, the advantages and the drawbacks before starting the investment portfolio.

CHAPTER FOUR

Crypto Coins And Their Potential In Investment

Cryptocurrencies were once considered to be a niche product suitable only for technical geeks and crypto enthusiasts, have now engulfed the whole world with their magic – 'the magic of making quick money.' This sudden craze in the financial world has not only been advantageous for the cryptocurrency market but has also been the reason for the rise of many fake crypto coins. It is true that the market is overflowing with too many cryptocurrencies making it hard for new and experienced investors to choose the right coin to their investment portfolio.

Though it is impossible to foresee the future of a specific cryptocurrency, it is always better to analyze their underlying technology and functionality to check which one would best suit your investment needs.

Crypto coins or Altcoins

Bitcoin is the commonly 'heard' word when it comes to cryptocurrency, and they go hand-in-hand in the crypto market with Bitcoin being the first and most valued cryptocurrency. We will not be discussing the coin for now as considering the current market table; Bitcoin is way too expensive to produce significant gain without having to take too much risk. Let us concentrate on the other cryptocurrencies that are suitable for investment in 2018:

- Ethereum
- Ripple
- Stellar
- IOTA
- Litecoin
- Neo

Ethereum

Ethereum is the second best popular cryptocurrency after Bitcoin and is currently well established in the crypto world. Ethereum is preferred over Bitcoin not only because of its crypto token 'Ether' but also due to the underlying technology, which is far more advanced in many ways. The concept of 'smart contract' has caught the attention of many investors – this blockchain platform (Ethereum platform) can help run more complex applications.

The mutual agreements which are used today for debts, investment contracts, etc. can be prepared in the Ethereum platform using the 'smart contracts' technology. Example: If you are investing a part of your allocation in a startup, you will have to divide the amount into parts as the company will not receive the entire money in one go but rather it would be invested in installments based on the company's growth milestone. This period division is documented in a contract with the help of advocates, notaries and other third-party experts, which adds to the cost factor of the investor. With Ethereum's smart contract option, the investor can hard-code the 'conditions' in the contract as in – when the next installment should be released, what is the milestone that is expected to be achieved, etc. This is then mutually agreed upon and triggered to action when the 'conditions are met' without any intervention.

The example makes it look simple, but the underlying technology is a bit more complex. However, the idea is remarkable. Ethereum is a platform which helps run business application whereas Bitcoin can be just used as a cryptocurrency. This is the reason many investors are overlooking Bitcoin for Ethereum. Apart from financial transactions, Ethereum platform provides a serious business solution.

Ethereum has already crossed its $1000 mark and is currently trading at $1050 with a total market cap of over $100 billion. Though this looks costly too, it is considered to be one of the safest bets in cryptocurrency market for this year 2018.

Ripple

Ripple's strong platform foundation makes it a good investment venue. Bitcoin was aimed with the sole intention of creating a decentralized economy without the need of any central regulatory body's intervention, but Ripple went a step ahead and informed the banking world that it is ready to work with them. The underlying blockchain technology used by Ripple allows international bank transactions in a fraction of second with strong security.

In January 2018, Ripple surpassed Ethereum to become the second leading crypto coin with respect to the market cap. This new coin 'Ripple' created a ripple in the cryptocurrency market when it traded at $3.06 with a total market cap of $118 billion. Its percentage value saw a tremendous increase of 37900% within 12 months from $0.0065 per coin in January 2017 to $2.47 per coin by the year-end.

Chris Larsen, Ripple's co-founder, became one of the wealthiest people in the world with $59.1 billion, due to this spectacular rise, leaving behind the likes of Google's Founders – Sergey Brin and Larry Page, which is overwhelming. On the whole, Ripple will make a good investment if you would like to get into the game of cryptocurrency.

Stellar

After Ripple, Stellar became the next blockchain platform ready to collaborate with banks to make international payment transactions easier for individuals and business firms. The application and idea it uses are the same, but the underlying technology is different when compared to ripple. Stellar has grown exponentially well to become one of the biggest cryptocurrencies with the rise of Ripple.

Lumen is the crypto token for the stellar platform, and this new blockchain platform has already circulated close to $8 billion lumens with its market capitalization rising to $13 billion. It is also considered to be the cheapest cryptocurrencies to invest as it is trading at 0.75$.

IOTA

IOTA's blockchain platform helps to concentrate on the future of the Internet of Things (IoT) and hence carries the name IOTA. This new cryptocurrency and its technology are too ahead of its time; this innovative concept has helped the currency to rise above 1000% in the last few months. IOTA's blockchain technology is referred to as 'Tangle.'

IOTA allows unlimited scalable payment system, i.e., it allows people to transfer funds with nil charges. This concept lets individuals and business firms to perform nano and microtransactions without any fee charges. The total market cap of IOTA is close to $12 billion, and it is being traded at $4.33, which definitely is a good investment for investors.

Litecoin

Charles Lee, a Google Engineer, created Litecoin in 2011 as an easy cryptocurrency, which offers a resource-friendly mining experience with quicker transactions and higher coin limit. Litecoin was the solution to the following problems produced by Bitcoin:

- Costly mining resources
- Slow transfer speed

Litecoin depends on 'individuals' to accept its technology whereas Stellar and Ethereum depends on business firms to accept their technology. The acceptance of the coin by the people was literally seen in Litecoin's growth percentage rate in 2017 – 1000% growth rates. The total market cap is over $16 billion and is currently trading at $299.95.

Neo

Neo is an open source project that is hosted on Github and was introduced in 2014. This Chinese blockchain based company is aiming to use blockchain technology and its digital characteristics to digitize physical assets, automate digital asset management using smart contracts and recognize 'smart economy' with a distributed network.

Digitizing the physical assets using a decentralized, noticeable, trustful and transparent blockchain technology without a third party intervention was the primary objective of Neo. There is a digital identity given to the owner of the asset which is generated using a set of X509 attuned digital identity standards, i.e., making the trading of physical assets easier and safer with less cost.

Neo is one of the fastest growing cryptocurrencies that is currently trading at $106.42 with a market cap of close to $6 billion. It is considered to be the safest bet as compared to the other crypto coins; the market volatility is quite stable.

Things to be done before you start with your cryptocurrency investment portfolio

Now that you have a clear understanding on the history of cryptocurrency, the technology it uses, the reason to invest in cryptocurrency, the pros and cons of the cryptocurrency and the various crypto coins available in the cryptocurrency market, it is time to get started with your investment portfolio. But before doing so, there are two important things to be done, and it is to choose the right:

- Cryptocurrency Exchange
- Cryptocurrency Wallet

Cryptocurrency Exchange

Cryptocurrency Exchange is the common online marketplace, which allows crypto investors to buy and sell their crypto coins using fiat currencies. Before choosing the right cryptocurrency exchange, it is important to look at the following:

- User-friendly platform
- Security and insurance provided in the exchange
- Trading volume
- Liquidity flow
- Maximum Purchase limits and Withdrawal limits
- Fees and Spreads available in detail.

The above-mentioned points will help you in reviewing the quality and dependability of the cryptocurrency exchange. Coinbase is known to be the best and most popularly used crypto exchange due to its excellent 100% crypto insurance and user-friendly interface.

You will first get registered in the Coinbase exchange, submit the necessary KYC and AML documents, choose your payment mode and link the same after which account verification is done. After successful registration, the below mentioned five steps would take you through the first crypto coin purchase:

(Bitcoin is taken as an example)

- Click the 'Buy/Sell Bitcoin' tab
- Click the drop-down menu and choose the payment method
- Type the amount you would want to invest
- Click 'Buy Bitcoin Instantly'
- Check for the credited Bitcoins on the Coinbase account dashboard.

And don't forget to check if your country and the relevant currency are supported by the exchange to help in smooth cryptocurrency transaction.

Cryptocurrency Wallets

Almost all the exchanges have an inbuilt online wallet to help the user store the crypto coin that has been purchased. But after the unfortunate theft incident with the exchange Mt. Gox, many investors are looking at offline wallets as they find it quite uncomfortable to have their crypto investments in an online wallet.

You can choose to have a paper wallet service by installing MyEtherWallet or use a hardware wallet like Trezor for storing your coins away from platform risk. But then it becomes your responsibility entirely to take care of your coins, and therefore it is advisable to use a two-factor authentication for safekeeping of your coins.

CHAPTER FIVE

Investing in Cryptocurrency

When you are investing your hard-earned money on a particular stock, the first and foremost thing you need to do is 'know what you are getting into.' Investing in cryptocurrency is no different from the usual traditional stocks or shares investment; the major factor is to understand the basics and its underlying technology. It is essential to be aware of the fact that when you are investing in any high speculative venture – be it traditional market stocks or the cryptocurrencies; you are always running into the risk of losing most of your investment (at least not all of it). So, it is crucial to follow the rule – *Don't invest an amount which you cannot afford to lose.*

The fact is, apart from a buyer's willingness to buy the cryptocurrency; this virtual currency doesn't hold any inherent value, which is the reason for large fluctuations in the price value that actually adds on to the risk percentage for the investor. If you are not ready to handle such high price swings, then it is better to not get into cryptocurrency.

What % of the investment allocation should be put in cryptocurrencies?

It is true that the market value is highly unpredictable and volatile when it comes to cryptocurrency but that shouldn't stop you from investing in these digital coins. You can definitely make good profits with the right investment strategy if you obviously know what you are doing and why you are doing it. As mentioned earlier, the basic thumb rule for cryptocurrency investment is, to invest a particular amount on the crypto coins only if you can afford to lose the money without getting into an emotional trauma. For example, if you have decided to allocate $500 to invest on Bitcoin, then go ahead with the said amount only if you are ready to lose the $500 in case the outcome turns out to be negative. If you feel $500 is way too much to lose, then better go for a lesser amount (maybe $100) so that even if you lose that money, you aren't emotionally affected by the loss.

Cryptocurrency investment doesn't come with any hard and fast rule, so it is completely on you to decide the investment allocation based on your current financial status and money-making goals. The following percentage allocation might help you with a basic idea on how to go about your first crypto investment portfolio:

- Let's say you are less than 30 years old; then you can have a combination of 50% traditional investment and 30% cryptocurrency investment
- If you fall under the age criteria between 30 and 40 years, it is advisable to go for 60% traditional investment and 20% cryptocurrency investment

- 70% traditional investment and 10% cryptocurrency investment if you are above 40 years old.

How to choose the right cryptocurrency?

There are so many crypto coins in the market and with a lot of people making suggestions, how is it even possible to make the right choice? The cryptocurrency is already high on the bull market, and anything could rise anytime. It is better to ask yourself the following questions before you decide on the cryptocurrency you would want to invest in:

Will I be able to maintain my capital amount?
Protecting your capital amount should be the first rule to be implemented. Check the reliability of the crypto coin. Do your research and find out if the cryptocurrency is genuine or is it a scam.

Does the coin I have chosen have a long-term plan?
Read the white paper of the cryptocurrency in their official website. Understand their concept and the underlying technology they use. Look for their mission statement. Identify if they have any long-term goals and if they are looking to achieve a particular milestone

Will the coin help with safety benefits?
Don't get carried away with their attractive web pages and advertisements. Check out for reviews. Most of the new coin developers would want to sell the coin and then vanish. You don't want to be their victim – so do your research. Go for reliable, trustworthy cryptocurrencies rather than looking at new coins that advertise about double the interest rates or huge profit figures.

Is your exit strategy ready?
Are you looking at long-term capital gains or short-term capital gains? Would you want to hold the coin for a particular period and trade it for fiat currency when the time is right? Or are you looking at holding the coin for a considerably longer period without worrying about the short-term price fluctuations? Devise the timeline and stick to it. Avoid taking a decision when you are at your emotional high.

Ways to make money!

There are various ways to make that extra bucks using cryptocurrency investment – be it on a long-term or short-term basis. If you were looking at a safe long-term investment plan, then the 'buy and hold' strategy would be the best way to gain a good amount of profit.

Buy and Hold
In this method, you can purchase the crypto coins and do nothing - but just hold on to it for a year or lesser. After the predetermined time, you can decide on selling the coin for fiat money or trading the coin for another crypto coin based on the value appreciation. Short-term price fluctuations, technical disturbances or other external factors shouldn't be a worrying aspect of this strategy. It is important to stay cool irrespective of the price oscillation and not end up 'panic selling' your crypto coins. Any decision taken when you are emotionally disturbed will result in huge losses.

Trading with Margin (Short-term)
If you are an experienced forex trader, you would want to try its methods in cryptocurrency too, like looking to trade on your 'stash' hoping to increase it but it is important to read between the lines of

the price value table before getting into it. Analyze the ups and downs of the price value by checking the trading history and try to predict the next expected 'highs and lows.' If you are a novice in cryptocurrency investment, it is essential to make a leveraged trade.

If you are brave enough to get into short-term trading without allowing your emotions to take control over you, then it is important to act fast, think wise and plan the next move.

Mining

Investors looking for passive income with long-term benefits with predictable returns can choose 'mining' as their option. The initial investment will be required to set the hardware for the mining process – the mining rig, high-speed processor, mining application software, mining pool, good amount of electricity and the right graphic card. It does take some effort in setting the environment up, but once you get the hang of it, it can be a good investment strategy. Not all cryptocurrencies can be mined – only the ones with 'Proof of Work' protocol can fall in the mining category.

Arbitraging with cryptocurrencies

Once you get a hold onto the cryptocurrency market and can understand the flow, you might want to make quick money - getting your hands on to multiple exchanges, buying from one exchange and selling on to another exchange to make 'arbitrage' gains. There are two major things you might want to consider when looking for the arbitraging break: fees factor and price change. When the price value keeps fluctuating, the price might keep changing when you transfer between exchanges thereby increasing the transaction fee.

How to start with Bitcoin investment?

The first step to start with Bitcoin investment is to buy the Bitcoin, and there are quite a number of cryptocurrency exchanges in the market to help you with the same. It is essential to do your own research while choosing the right exchange.

Coinbase is said to be the most popular one among the various other exchanges in the market, and this secondary exchange gives 1% markup to the customer for selling their Bitcoins. It also offers an automatic buy option which allows the customer to purchase Bitcoins for a particular value regularly on a monthly basis, i.e., the investor can set up the dates on which they would want the exchange to automatically buy the coin at a particular value, like 7th of every month to initiate the Bitcoin request. The money required for the Bitcoin will get auto-debited from the bank account that has been linked to the exchange.

But the drawback in this option is, the investor will not have control on the price value of the Bitcoin, which might sometime cross the budget that has been allocated for the investment portfolio since the price value keeps fluctuating almost on a regular basis.

Once you have your Bitcoin safely stored in your wallet, decide on the investment strategy and keep studying the market value, trading charts and price fluctuations to know when to make the next move.

Securing the cryptocurrencies

It is crucial to store the purchased cryptocurrencies in a secured way away from scammers and hackers by using the right coin wallets. Choose a trusted digital coin wallet in the cryptocurrency market and transfer the purchased crypto coins from the online exchange wallets to your offline digital coin wallets.

The development of hardware wallets is completely based on its security level, and hence most of the crypto investors choose paper wallets or hardware wallets to store their crypto coins. Trezor is a popularly used hardware wallet, which generates its private key in offline mode. Ledger Nano S is a reliable Bitcoin wallet with strong security levels.

CHAPTER SIX

Cryptocurrency Investment strategies

The previous chapter would have helped you understand the different modes of cryptocurrency investment and the ways to go about it. To decide on the right investment plan; it is important to devise the best investment strategies which would help you to choose the right crypto coin, make sure to avoid repeated mistakes, understand the various methods to store the crypto coins, etc.

Investment strategy for Cryptocurrency

It is the calculated decision of the investor to invest in cryptocurrency, which has its own set of risks and rewards considering the market volatility and its unpredictable price fluctuations. Analyzing the market based on its previous track records, understanding the trade charts and deciding on the right coin to invest will help you create a strategic investment plan to help you get into the game of cryptocurrency. This process of working out on a strategic plan is referred to as the investment strategy for the cryptocurrency.

How much should I invest on cryptocurrency? On what basis should I be choosing the right coin? How to choose the best investment plan to gain better returns? Will it be easy to cash out on the cryptocurrency? Is there a particular time to buy or sell the crypto coin? If you have decided to go ahead with cryptocurrency investment, then these are the possible questions that would come to your mind.

The investor should have a clear plan on what he would be doing after he buys his crypto coin, he should also have an idea on how long he will be holding on to the coin before he converts it to fiat currency, etc. The two major factors to be noted when it comes to cryptocurrency investment are:

- Devising a strategic plan
- Picking the best investment strategy

Ask yourself the following questions to start your cryptocurrency investment portfolio:

- Have you decided on the amount you would be allocating for cryptocurrency investment?
- Why do you choose to invest in cryptocurrency? Is there a reason behind the same?
- Would you be able to afford to lose the capital investment amount if it doesn't work out as planned?
- Are you looking to make quick money?
- Or are you looking for a long-term investment that would benefit you with long-term capital gains?
- Would you prefer to 'hold' on to your cryptocurrency?
- Do you have plans of diversifying your investment approach or do you want to stick to one cryptocurrency?

The answers to these questions will help you devise the right investment strategy putting you on the right track.

The safest and easiest way to invest in cryptocurrency is by following the long-term investment strategy as it attracts lesser transaction fees because you don't need to get involved in regular trading and the risk factor is less compared to the other investment strategies.

The most important investment strategy is to – purchase the right crypto coin at the right time. It is advisable to buy the coin when the price is low and sell when the price value goes up. Don't make the mistake of buying a crypto coin when its price value is really high with an assumption that you can make big bucks by selling the coin in the next few days. This is the traditional stock market approach and will not work with cryptocurrency, as the market is extremely volatile. You should wait for at least a month to trade your coin if it is a short-term investment and in case of long-term investment, it is necessary to hold on to the coin between six months to one year.

Buying the coin when the price value is steady is also a good idea, i.e., the price value will neither be too high nor be too low but will have a low differential spread.

Steps to be followed for the right investment strategy

The best investment strategy comes after making a calculative decision based on your current financial status and the estimated profit returns you are expecting from the portfolio. You will be able to enjoy the benefits you had expected out of the plan and would also be capable of staying in the market much longer than you had expected initially. The below-mentioned steps would help you choose the right investment strategy for your cryptocurrency portfolio:

Working out on the right plan to start your investment portfolio

The amount you have allocated for investing should be the base for choosing the right crypto coin. The chosen coin should adhere to your requirements and satisfy your moneymaking goals – so it is essential to make a realistic profit expectation and understand the limitations in the same. Do your research in such a way that you are able to analyze the price value of the coin, study its previous track record and understand its trading charts that would help you predict the price fluctuations. Though this comes in by experience, it is never too late to learn the same. This would help you with an exit strategy when the time is up.

Be ready to accept the 'price dips'

You will need to be prepared to acknowledge and identify the price dip of the cryptocurrencies once you have decided to get into cryptocurrency investment. This price fluctuation does happen for a reason, and when you are smart enough to find the same, that is when you win! These may be the basic reasons for price dips:

The reason for the price dip of one crypto coin might be due to the increase in price value of another crypto coin – mostly its competitor or the coins with similar features. Vice versa is also possible

- Rumors and unauthenticated news in the media can be one of the reasons for the price dips
- Media broadcasting news on cryptocurrencies can alter the course of its price value thereby creating a disturbance in the market. For instance, if there is a news which says 'stellar's

price increase led to the price value decrease in ripple', then investors might 'panic sell' their ripple coins and new investors might rush to stellar for starting a new investment which in a way will alter the price values of both the coins.
- A country's decision on banning cryptocurrencies will also result in an overall performance dip on the crypto tables' value.

Keeping your cool in such circumstances will definitely save you from heavy losses.

Securing the cryptocurrencies

The key factor of cryptocurrency investment is to keep the crypto coins safe and secure. Unlike fiat currencies, computers create cryptocurrencies in a digitized format, and it is susceptible to security risks such as virus attacks, cyber threats, thefts, etc. When it comes to traditional banking approach, you always have the option of getting new credentials in case you forget your password or can contact the bank officials if you lose your credit or debit card and request them to block the card to prevent it from unauthorized transactions.

But with cryptocurrencies, there are no such options and hence if you lose your private key, then it means you have lost your crypto coins. You don't have any way to retrieve it back; it is gone - once and for all. Similarly, if the coins you had stored in the online wallet of a cryptocurrency exchange get stolen, then there is no way to track it back as blockchain technology offers anonymity. Transferring the coin to the wrong wallet address will also result in losing the transferred coins, and you don't have any possibility of getting the coin back unless the recipient is courteous enough to return it to you

All these reasons zeroes down to the fact that –it is crucial to store your cryptocurrency in a secured manner and the most advised option is to use hardware wallet or paper wallet for coin storage and take a backup of the .dat file of the cryptocurrency. It is good to apply two-factor authorization for doubling up the security.

Making money

Since the beginning of 2017, the ROI (return of investment) on cryptocurrency has risen up to 900%, and it is impossible to see such huge rise in ROIs of traditional investment methods – stocks, shares, bonds, etc. The long-term investment strategy with cryptocurrency comes with unbelievable gains, as the 'figure' is mind-boggling.

In traditional investment market, the investor will have to hold on to his or her stocks for at least three years or more before making money out of it but when it comes to cryptocurrency, the 'holding period' is reduced to a year or lesser considering the cryptocurrency market which moves exceedingly fast with its price value volatility. For instance, if you had invested $500 on Bitcoins at the beginning of the year, there is a high possibility of gaining returns equal to $5000 by the end of the year.

Buying small fractions of the coins when the price is low and holding on to it for a certain period before selling it is known as 'buying the dips.' There are two ways to do it:

- Buy the coins at regular intervals every time the price goes down.
- Buy the coin when the price settles down i.e., there might have been a price value decrease a few days back, and then it would have again increased and then would have come to a figure that is in between the last decrease and the last increase.

It would finally settle down at that spread for few days. Buy the coin then.

'Buying the dips' comes in two ways – '*buy the little dips*' and '*buy the big dips.*'

Buying the coin when the price goes down from its last value is referred as *buying the little dips*. Buying the coin when the price completely goes down to a steep low (below the average), then it is *buying the big dips.*

When to use the dips?
- If you have chosen the 'buy and hold' investment strategy, then you can 'buy the big dip' to help you create a long-term cryptocurrency investment portfolio
- If you are choosing a short-term investment strategy and going for range trading, then you can 'buy the little dips'

When to sell?
The one and only rule to sell is – Sell the crypto coin only when the price value is high. There is no alternative way to this. *Buy low and sell high!*

It is good to keep a track record of the price value fluctuations for every hour, week, month, quarter and six months. This exercise would help you to decide when to buy and when to sell. It might also help you to predict the next price value increase or decrease (this comes with experience).

Cryptocurrency

Inspiration from a Bitcoin millionaire

Erik Finman, the 19-year-old Bitcoin millionaire, says even $1000 from your investment allocation is enough to invest in cryptocurrency. This young man has been lucky with his cryptocurrency investment and has turned a millionaire with just $1000 as his initial investment in the age of 12. He purchased his first Bitcoin when he was 12 and became a millionaire by 18. Erik is the owner of 401 Bitcoins whose net worth is $3.4 million ($8512 per coin).

The advice he gives to his fellow cryptocurrency investors is – "Invest 10 percent of your income on cryptocurrencies". According to him, Bitcoin is the safest bet when it comes to cryptocurrency as of now. The price value of Bitcoin reached $16000 in the first week of February 2018.

It is safe to follow the 50-30-20 rule where '50 percent of the income goes to necessities, 30 percent goes to non-compulsive spending and the remaining 20% of the income should be towards saving.' Now all your investment and trading portfolio comes under this 20% saving umbrella as irrespective of the investment style you follow, the objective of investing is to 'save for the future.'

Now if you are going to follow Finman's suggestion, then out of this 20% - you should try to build a diversified investment portfolio where 10% should be for cryptocurrency investment and the remaining 10% to 'other investment portfolio based on your financial status.'

The teenage millionaire also adds a disclaimer to his statement, which is – "Only invest what you are willing to lose."

CHAPTER SEVEN

Cryptocurrency Exchanges

By now you would have got a brief idea about cryptocurrency investments and the various investment strategies which would help you to make that extra money you have always wanted to. It is indeed time to begin your journey with these crypto coins – Ether, Litecoin, Bitcoin, etc. and make your financial position a bit stronger than what it is now. To make this possible, you will first need a suitable cryptocurrency exchange – this will help to convert your fiat money (dollars, pounds, rupees, etc.) into cryptocurrencies (Bitcoin, ether, ripple, Litecoin, etc.)

Cryptocurrency exchange is an online marketplace platform that acts a bridge between the crypto buyers and sellers. It allows both the parties to buy or sell the crypto coins through different payment modes – using fiat money to buy the cryptocurrency or trade an existing cryptocurrency with a new cryptocurrency, i.e., XBT/USD (Bitcoin and US dollars) or XBT/ETH (Bitcoin and Ether).

The traditional stock exchange market allows the traders to buy new stocks and sell existing shares or stocks based on the market rate values mentioned in the stock table. Similarly, cryptocurrency exchanges allow the crypto enthusiasts to buy and sell cryptocurrencies based on the price value table.

The cryptocurrency exchange allows the traders to choose 'market order' option that permits the exchange to trade the crypto coins for the best-offered price in the market. Similarly, when the trader chooses the 'limit order' option, the exchange is directed to trade the cryptocurrencies for a much lower price than the 'current ask' or the 'current bid' for buying and selling.

How to choose the right cryptocurrency exchange?

Majority of the cryptocurrency enthusiasts had become more cautious while choosing the right cryptocurrency exchange after the Japanese based cryptocurrency exchange 'Mt Gox' was hacked and its users lost all their cryptocurrencies that were stored in the particular exchange. It was even more alarming when more news kept coming up about security breaches in exchange; theft of crypto coins, etc. and all these forced the people to be more careful on cryptocurrency exchanges.

Try asking the following questions to self before you finalize on a particular cryptocurrency exchange:

- Does the cryptocurrency exchange have enough security measures to keep the platform safe from external attacks?
- Does the exchange have high liquidity flow?
- Does the exchange provide all the necessary data requested by the user? Price value, transaction volume, charges, etc.?
- Does the exchange support enough currencies – at least the major ones?
- Are there multiple payment options available? Cards, PayPal, banking, wire transfers, etc.?

- Does the exchange have good reviews and is it one of the most sorted ones in the market?
- Is the platform beginner-friendly?

If you get satisfying answers to the above queries, then don't worry you have just got hold of the right cryptocurrency exchange. The exchange should be suitable to the investor on the following:

- Ease of transaction
- Less transaction time
- Safe coin storage
- Simple and quick

Why is it important to choose a safe cryptocurrency exchange?

Cryptocurrency transactions are irreversible, and this makes it important to choose the right and secure cryptocurrency exchange. Sending the coin to a wrong wallet address, failing to keep the coin safe resulting in theft, allowing the wallet to get attacked by phishing scams, etc. are few of the major mistakes most cryptocurrency users make.

Doing thorough research on the popular cryptocurrency exchanges available in the market and choosing the best ones suiting your investment needs is very crucial. Most critics advise the investors not to store their untouched cryptocurrencies (the coins which are not used for trading but just stored 'to hold') in the online wallet of a cryptocurrency exchange. There is always a risk of getting attacked by cyber thieves or the platform going down for various reasons or possible chance of security breach. In such cases, there is no way to get your crypto coins. It is gone forever!

And don't forget to go through their transaction fee structure before finalizing the exchange, as you don't want to end up paying more money as charges for the transaction than the actual profit you make.

Don't make these investment mistakes

Now that you have worked out your investment plan, selected the right investment strategy, finalized on the cryptocurrency exchange which is suiting your needs; you can get started with your cryptocurrency investment portfolio. Wait for a second! Before getting into the ground, there is a last step to be done. When you have decided to put your hard-earned money into cryptocurrency, then it is vital to ensure you don't end up making the same 'old mistakes' your seniors had made.

It is best to avoid the below-mentioned mistakes so that you don't get a nervous breakdown because of the monetary losses:

- Don't spend the entire capital amount on one particular crypto coin. Take it slow and begin your portfolio with a small investment. As you see positive outcomes, gradually increase the investment amount. As you gain experience, try to invest in more than one cryptocurrency (but don't forget to do the research for the same). *Avoid putting all the apples in one basket.*

- It is important to diversify your investment portfolio. Don't get too obsessed with cryptocurrency; invest a part of the allocation to traditional investment method too. Spread the investment volume suiting your financial needs – take note of the risks involved, the estimated profit expectation, the waiting time, etc. *Don't be possessive with your crypto assets.*
- As you very well know that the cryptocurrency market is extremely volatile, it is essential to take control of the situation – think logically and avoid taking decisions when you are controlled by your own emotions. Don't go 'panic selling' your coins when the price value drops. *Avoid getting restless during price dips.*
- Don't lose all your investment, keep some safe, i.e., remember to keep few crypto coins safe in your hardware wallet while you are busy making profits by trading the remaining ones. *Always leave some coins behind.*
- Buy when the price is low
- Focus on the coin circulation; market value and the total market cap rather than concentrating too much on the unit price of the crypto coin.
- Day trading is not suitable for the cryptocurrency; it is too dangerous. Until you are experienced enough to read between the lines of market fluctuations, it is better to stick to 'buy and hold' strategy. I know it gets too tempting when you see experienced traders boasting about the millions they made in day trading but remember if you are not careful to make the right decision quickly at the perfect time, you can end up losing 'big figures.'
- Cryptocurrency investment strategy completely depends on the individual, and there is no specific strategy to be followed.

A strategy that worked for me might not necessarily work for you. This is where devising the strategic plan comes into picture – it is crucial to work out your plan based on your financial requirement, money making goal, tax liabilities, etc
- Don't get overconfident because you made triple profits more than once; it doesn't make you an expert. Relax and take it slow!
- The most crucial part – *Don't invest the amount if you cannot afford to lose it.*

Since Bitcoin has been introduced, it continues to be the 'hot topic of debate' when the future of cryptocurrency is discussed. In spite of the price value fluctuations and various other issues that the first coin had to face, Bitcoin still continues to be a successful cryptocurrency and has been an inspiration to develop many new alternative cryptocurrencies such as Litecoin, Ripple, Ethernet, etc. If the cryptocurrency needs to become a part of the mainstream fiscal system, it will need to satisfy the conflicting critics and emerge as a widely accepted currency.

Though the possibility looks distant, there is the slightest doubt that the success or failure of Bitcoin while dealing with its own challenges may definitely determine the destiny of all the other cryptocurrencies in the upcoming years.

CONCLUSION

We have come to the end of this book. I would like to take this opportunity to thank you once again for choosing this book - *"Cryptocurrency: Investment strategies in 2018."*

I sincerely hope this book was useful and helped you as a reader to understand the history of cryptocurrency, the reason behind its evolution and the popular cryptocurrencies that are currently available. This book was written with the intent to give readers a detailed description of the advantages and disadvantages of the cryptocurrencies and the various investment potentials it holds. There is a chapter that deals with the popular cryptocoins in the market and their potential to be the source of investment for your cryptocurrency investment portfolio this 2018.

The book has covered the primary objective, which is to give the readers an in-depth functional knowledge of cryptocurrency, its underlying technology, the various cryptocurrency investments and the best possible ways to make money using them. The book also gives a quick overview of the concept of cryptocurrency exchanges and the cryptocurrency investment strategies to be considered.

With so many cryptocurrencies available in the market, it is entirely in the hands of the cryptocurrency investors to choose the right coins that will suit their investment and financial needs. This book will help you understand the various investment strategies and the ways to implement them into your own strategic plan.

I sincerely hope this book was useful and has helped in answering the queries you had in mind. My best wishes to you for making the best out of the cryptocurrency market by working out a strategic plan that best suits you and helps you in choosing the best cryptocurrency investment strategy.

Thank you and best wishes!

BONUS!

Because you have bought my book I have one more bonus for you

I want to give you full access to a bonus page with the EXTRA TOP WALLETS for your crypto business for FREE , simply as a "thank you" for downloading this book.

Also, get notified when my new books go on a free promotion and get FREE BOOKS from subscribing to my email.

If you are someone who is interested in saving a ton of money, then simply click the link for free ACCESS.

CLICK HERE FOR INSTANT ACESS

http://eepurl.com/dl0V5v

Thank you

www.ingramcontent.com/pod-product-compliance
Lightning Source LLC
Chambersburg PA
CBHW070415230526
45471CB00006B/2824